Drunken Boxing:
Breaking Through to Advanced Practice

By: Shifu Daniel Schultz

Table of Contents

Disclaimer: Before Letting Go, You Must Have Something to Let Go.   4

Tree doesn't try to Root or Stand   9

From One came Two, from Two came Three, from Three came Ten Thousand Things   13

Rules are a Prison   20

Letting Go   25

Let Go of Feeling Power   29

Let Go of how it Looks   32

Let Go of Shape   36

Let Go of Form   38

Let Go of Root   40

Let Go of Structure   43

Let go of Control/Self   45

Let go of mind/body   49

First there is Shape, Let Go of Shape, There Never was a Shape   52

Yin/Yang Reversal   55

Yin/Yang Exist Together   58

Yin/Yang Disappear   60

There are 8 Immortals   62

Imitation vs Embodying   66

There are 9 Immortals	68
There is only One Immortal	70
Rule of Xu: Everybody Sucks, do the Opposite	72
Change the Self	75
Emptiness	79
Self vs Non Self	81
Emptiness and Martial Arts	82
Emptiness and Drunken Boxing	85
Enlightenment: Seeing Things that were there Before	87
Enlightenment: Opening the Mind, Changing the Nervous System	89
Practice a Style, Remove the Style, "The Art" Remains	92
Don't Try to be your Teacher, be You	95
Imitation vs Embodying 2	99
Conclusion	102

Disclaimer: Before Letting Go, You Must Have Something to Let Go.

I feel I should mention very early in this book, the things I will be covering here are more advanced topics. As such those who are at the beginning of their martial journey may not find much use for this book until some time later. Or worse yet they may find it incredibly useful and start the advanced practices without having a thorough foundation within the beginner to intermediate practices. One cannot build a house without proper foundations to hold it in place.

In this book, I will talk about things like "letting go." Letting go of shapes, letting go of form, becoming shapeless and formless. But it is important to practice and establish shape and form before this practice. In order to let go of something, you must have it to begin with. If I want to put down a pen, I must pick it up in the first place. In order to let go of a deep sadness from a relative passing away, I must first acknowledge and embrace those feelings. Then they can be let go and we move on.

I understand the allure of advanced practices. I too was attracted to advanced level skills before I was ready. It's a very human thing to do. We're attracted to the big shiny new thing. But it is important to put into perspective that advanced principles are not "new" principles. Rather they are extensions and continuations of the basic principles we were taught as beginners. Thus if we don't have proper training in the foundations, we can never truly understand the advanced principles. Before we learn to make sentences, we must first learn the alphabet and make words. Before we learn to run, first we must walk. We cannot skip stages, or we break everything.

But what would happen if we were to skip stages? First off we wouldn't grasp the concept in the first place and thus would be clueless. Second, we likely would create "false positives." Faking our way into thinking we have something special. Third, likely we would create massive egos. The thing about high level martial arts is that it's a lot of hard work. Not only in the advanced stages, but in the stages to get there. This kind of work trains and expands the mind along with working the body. The more the mind is expanded, the more we can see and realize that we still have so much to learn. This tends to create a sense of humility in those that have made it to the advanced levels, as they realize the hard work it takes and that they themselves are not special for making it to where they are. Even more so they see that they still have much to learn and so will continually strive to better themselves.

But those who skip the hard work in the beginning stages and start working on the advanced stuff right away create their false feedback. This feedback will make them believe that they have skills that they do not possess. Yi Ling Qi Means, "Mind (intent) leads the Qi (relationships)." In short it means "Mind over Matter." One very important thing to remember about this phrase that my teacher's Kung Fu brother put into perspective, that phrase is not instructions, it's the warning label. Though we use the mind to affect the body in practice, we must be wary of what we are thinking. If the mind can help and bolster the body by the way we think, then it can tear us down and make us crazy as well.

Qigong Bing (Qigong sickness) is a very real thing. Its symptoms and effects can vary from tangible sicknesses with heat or cold symptoms, to intangible symptoms in the way it affects the mind. A type of Qigong bing, the one I am discussing here, is a distortion of reality. Basically craziness. Picture this scenario. You are stuck in a room, and your only view to the outside world is a single window. At first, you can see clearly out the window, but over time if the window is not being cleaned, it collects phlegm and dirt. What once appeared as a mailbox now looks like a stalker. What was once a tree is now a demon. This kind of Qigong bing is a change to how the mind views reality. Seeing things that aren't actually there. Particularly in our case of creating false positives in training, making ourselves believe we are better than we are. When our view of reality doesn't match reality, then we are sick and seeing the world through our own bias.

This kind of false outlook can lead us to becoming very egotistical people. Think about it. The practitioner who has gone through the work and layers of training has become humble because he knows the road is difficult and he sees his own faults through the training he has endured. But those that skip the layers and create their false positives have not gone through the grueling training. They have not found the faults in themselves and have not worked on them through the training. So they don't know they have those faults to begin with. To add more, they didn't go through the work to get to the advanced stages and simply jumped ahead to the shiny advanced practices. Instead of following a long grueling path, it's like they found the "secrets," and thus they are special because they know something many others don't know. To "keep secrets" in this way is a way to fuel the ego and hold a carrot in front of potential students and trick them into thinking you know more than you do.

Everybody wants to feel special and unique. It's a very human thing to do. So many will hold such teachings in a way that will put themselves on a pedestal to be admired. But while it's a nice feeling and is understandable why people pursue such things, it creates a complete halt of progression. The real practitioners are walking the path constantly, not halting to be admired. We must move forward, or there is no point.

So I hope this chapter makes it clear that this book is going to be focusing on the advanced topics of martial arts through the view of drunken boxing, and not everyone may get something out of it right away. I chose to write this book as this level of discussion about martial arts is rarely talked about, and even more rarely understood. And while I don't want to say beginners can't learn something from this book, I also want to not screw up someone's martial journey by saying these advanced topics should be studied at beginning levels. The topics here should be more carefully looked at after some serious training has already taken place. I hope everyone gets something out of this book. Anyway, that's my disclaimer, on to the good stuff.

Tree doesn't try to Root or Stand

In martial arts we train many skills over and over, again and again until we can do them without thinking about it anymore. When we can do things innately, conscious action is no longer required. This is what many refer to as "do without doing" or "regulate without regulating." These paradoxes serve to describe this unconscious, instinctive, innate level of doing any practice. Typically when learning to drive, we focus a lot on the many various components of learning to drive. How to start the car. How to steer. How much do we need to turn the wheel, turn more or turn less. How far down do we press the gas pedal and how far in advance should we start applying the breaks. It's a lot to think about.

But eventually through practice and experience we get used to driving and these things happen instinctively. So no longer do we spend a lot of our time thinking about them, but instead we focus on the road ahead and the traffic to keep ourselves going in the right direction and safe from obstacles. This theory applies to anything we do and martial arts is no exception.

So now looking through the lens of drunken boxing, drunken boxing assumes you already have a set of skills to work with. There is a reason it is referred to as an advanced form of martial arts. And it is not at all because it can be athletic. Sometimes drunken boxing even appears in other systems or styles as a single form taught late in a practitioner's training. So by the time you learn it, you already have plenty of martial arts to work with and build on. The way drunken works is to change one's thinking. To take the rules and principles that we learned in any art and bend them until they break, dial it back one notch, and then train in that space. Dancing on the line and finding the limits of our art and in doing so, find what makes those principles work in the first place. Because once we find out "why" it works, then we can be much more flexible and free with how we apply it which makes it easier to learn to adapt to change well. Otherwise we remain rigid through self-imposed limitations, and that makes it easy for opponent's to take advantage of our rigid minds. A rigid, closed mind is easily picked apart and offended by new information.

So all this goes to show the importance of proper foundations to work with. Not only that, but to make them innate. Because we can practice endlessly, but if the skills still require conscious thought to perform, then when we switch to drunken training we will break the rules entirely. It is important to remember that drunken bends and twists the rules, but never fully breaks them. So they must be a part of our being just as walking is.

In martial arts, we often talk about the concept of rooting. Rooting is a metaphor often used for training stability and groundedness. With good root, we are not easily knocked off balance. Now ask the question, do trees need to root? Do trees need to consciously ground themselves to keep from falling over? No, they do not need to think such things. They are trees. Rooting into the ground is a natural part of their being. They root without needing to root. So we should be the same. We train root, until we have root. Then we don't need to train to root anymore, because it happens all on its own. Any martial principle should be trained to this point. It's what really makes improving possible in the first place. In one phase of practice I may practice rooting. When that becomes innate, it becomes time to let go of the conscious decision to root and let it do it on its own. This frees up our mind to focus on another principle until that one also becomes instinctive. It is very difficult to focus on things like storing and releasing power when our mind is 50% split between thinking about that and thinking about rooting.

He who chases two rabbits catches none, but he who chases one rabbit catches two. One and then the other. If you cannot let go of the second rabbit while chasing the first, you won't catch the first rabbit. If you are chasing the second rabbit but still thinking about the first rabbit you've caught, then you'll be too distracted to realize the second rabbit changed directions long ago and is miles away by now. It is important to let go. To quote the Dao De Jing, "10,000 things rise and fall without cease, creating without possessing. Working without taking credit. Work is done, then forgotten. Therefore it lasts forever."

From One came Two, from Two came Three, from Three came Ten Thousand Things

無極 Wuji   太極 Taiji   An older Taiji symbol

There are many diagrams and tables in Chinese culture as well as martial arts to explain phenomena and in martial arts case, concepts, principles, and theories. "From one came the two." This refers to wuji becoming yin/yang, or taiji as it was referred to. In one way this was to describe the universe before and after the big bang. Wuji(無極) or "no extremity" is the universe before. It is describing a void that is filled with potential to transform. My teacher called it, "pregnant with potential." Though there was nothing, the potential to become something and transform was there and was ready. Big bang happens and it created taiji(太極) or grand extremity interchange. Yin/Yang literally meaning dark/bright is the concept used to categorize everything in the universe to make sense of it. By categorizing everything into supposed opposites, things can be compared and contrasted to make sense. We only have a concept of day, because night is its contrast. Otherwise day would be the norm and we wouldn't need a concept to categorize it. But the further we look into things, the less black and white it becomes. Thus the saying, "There is yin inside yang, and yang inside yin." The time when the day is most yin is midnight, and the time when it is most yang is noon. But all the times in between are variations of yin/yang. As we approach midnight the yang percentage decreases and yin increases. But the moment midnight hits and the day is at its most yin, it immediately begins the process of decreasing in yin and increasing in yang. So there is not only yin or yang, but there are varying percentages and they are constantly changing.

"From the two came the three, from the three came the ten thousand things." The two being the concept of yin and yang. The third is the concept of taiji which is the interchange of yin/yang. The "ten thousand things" is all that comes after and is built off of yin/yang. Yin/yang essentially encompasses everything, but we as humans have a hard time being okay with broad brush strokes and we like to examine things in great detail and specificity. So other charts were created to look at things with more detail.

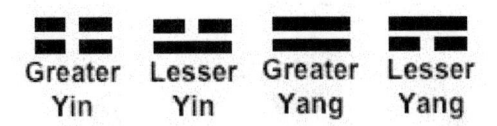

Greater Lesser Greater Lesser
Yin   Yin   Yang   Yang

To go over some of them quickly, we have the 4 directions showing variations of yin/yang in 4 pairs. Double yin, double yang, yang over yin, and yin over yang.

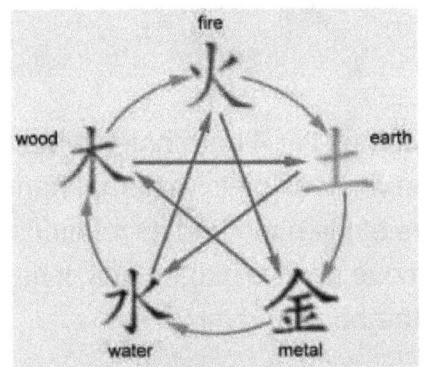

Then we have the 5 elements (more correctly titled as 5 phases) showing 5 powers. Fire, water, earth, metal, and wood. With both the creation and destruction cycle in the chart it shows that anything affecting one of these affects them all, whether through destruction or healing. Xingyiquan is known for using this chart.

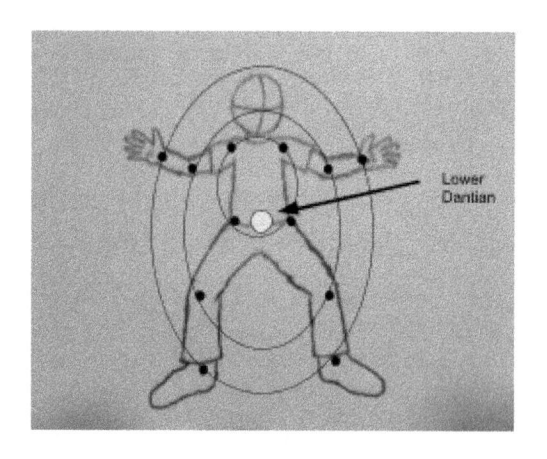

Then comes the 6 harmonies when broken down are 3 pairings of joints (external harmonies), and the harmonies of the mind and its relationship to the body as we move and do martial arts. It has a lot to do with moving the body and mind.

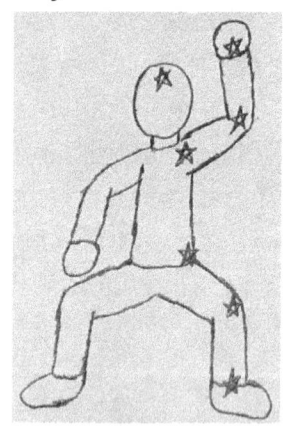

Next is the 7 stars which is looked at differently across martial arts. The 7 stars are referring to the big dipper. In some arts it refers to a stepping pattern, in others it is about the body's surface areas for hitting. Fist, elbow, shoulder, foot, knee, hip, and head.

16

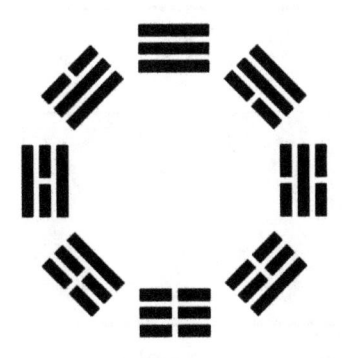

Then comes then 8 trigrams, or bagua(八卦). Bagua like the 4 directions, uses variations of yin/yang, but uses 3 lines in 8 variations. It is once again categorizing further the variations of yin/yang. Yin being broken lines and yang being solid lines, we get 3 lines on top of each other, and we get 8 variations from this. Bagua is about change. The mistake would be to assume that bagua is about these trigrams themselves. But Bagua actually refers to the space in between. Bagua is the change from one gua (trigram) to another. To further emphasize this point, Baguazhang (a martial art based on the theory of bagua) uses a stepping pattern called "9 Palace Stepping," to further integrate the idea of change.

4	9	2
3	5	7
8	1	6

    Where bagua has a palm change for every gua to illustrate each change, 9 palaces use a grid on the ground to represent the changes and as they walk and change direction, they change to embody the gua they are walking toward. But while the palm changes have multiple movements before walking the circle and moving on, the 9 palaces have you changing so quickly, you don't have time to embody that change for long before you must change again.

    So now if we compare this to learning martial arts, first we have nothing. We suck, and our instincts reflect our inexperience. But we have the potential to change that. We can learn and become better. So we embody wuji. Empty, but filled with potential. We start training. We learn some basics, some patterns and drills. We start to have material to compare and contrast. This is taiji. As we continue we start to build on those foundations. We start learning techniques, building shapes, learning the foundations of power, etc. We keep building and eventually we obtain lots of material. Concepts and theories are hard to understand without examples to look at. So to learn the important concepts, we learn many techniques. These are our examples to look at and study the principles. Some of us need more examples than others to get the points across, so some systems even include ludicrous amounts of forms and techniques. This of course is not wrong. Again, every human is different. Some of us need more. This is the ten thousand things.

But the more we continue to learn martial arts, we eventually do this process over again in reverse. We learn many techniques, but they can be summed up into principles, concepts, theories, and variations of change. Eventually we can take ten thousand techniques and narrow it down to 8 variations of change, thus the bagua. Then we can further simplify it and realize that the 8 variations are really just variations of yin/yang. We may come down to 8 tactics, but in the end everything is just circles. Thin, wide, spiralling, etc. They rotate one direction or the other. All the theories and concepts get summed up as the basics we learned in the beginning. Advanced concepts are just basics looked at through the lens of an experienced mind. We return to taiji. All of these things we train eventually become second nature. We no longer have to think about them, because we already embody them. Everything returns to wuji. You no longer have to think to root, nor how to throw a punch, you just do it. Training after that is just refinement. Once we return to wuji, that's where real training begins.

Rules are a Prison

So now after having learned martial arts for some time we are left with these principles and rules to follow. Now these principles we embody in ourselves are no longer consciously thought about and we simply do automatically. This is where drunken boxing training really begins. Now comes time to break the rules, or more accurately bend the rules until they break, dial it back a hair and train in that space. This is why drunken boxing is a style reserved more for people who already have a martial arts background. The style assumes you already have a set of rules and principles to play with. In many cases styles have a single drunken form in their curriculum that is trained last as an advanced practice. This comes from a realization that one can become too rigid in following the rules that it inhibits the practitioner, so drunken boxing is used to make the practitioner's mind flexible so it can flow. Looking at it, the more one trains drunken boxing, the more they can flow as their body learns to relax and become flexible. And as the body becomes flexible, the mind follows suit. As the mind

20

realizes that we can flow better when relaxed, the mind can relax and become flexible as well.

So this idea of stretching the principles until they break. If I take a principle and see how far I can bend and twist it, eventually it will break. But in doing so I can find that point where it does break and no longer work. Then by dialing it back a notch and practicing in that space it teaches us that these rules can stretch a lot further and still work than we realize. We will eventually find that these rules are here to guide us to the destination, not limit us as we practice. So I will take a couple principles or rules from some styles and use them as examples.

Standing straight and alignment principles from arts like taijiquan. This is about aligning the bones in a way so that gravity can hit our bodies and transfer through our feet to the ground with no joint being out of line to create obstruction which in cases can lead to pains in places like the lower back if the tailbone is out of alignment or the knees if they are positioned wrong. In doing this we also make it easier to ground ourselves from an opponent trying to throw or uproot us as we already have proper alignment to take and receive force. In drunken boxing, it is no secret that there are many times when the practitioner appears to have broken this rule, but if they actually know what they are doing, they still have the benefits of alignment even when not straight. I'd like to introduce the term verticality. While alignment physically aligns the bones to accept force, verticality is the implied line through the body to accept force even if the body is not straight. So we see positions like "drunkard lifts the barrel" and it is immediately obvious it is not straight by the bent over backward posture. But done correctly it has verticality. The practitioner first has their hips pulled forwards rather than simply leaning backward and it keeps the chest over the hips. The tailbone does not point back and instead points down as Ming men point on the lower back tries to face the earth. The center of the chest presses upward toward the sky. This alleviates pressure on the lower back and creates an arch position. Done correctly and someone should even be able to stand on the practitioner's chest as they stand like this. (Don't try at home without professional guidance) So we see that even though the practitioner is not aligned, he still has the benefits gained from alignment.

      Some styles have a rule to never kick above the waist. This is meant to lessen the chance that an opponent can grab the foot and take advantage. So now if we apply the drunken mindset, we try kicking above the waist. We'll find that it is true that doing so exposes us to more danger. However if we experiment with partners in sparring and accept the idea that we are probably going to eat it more than usual and still make use of high kicks anyway, every time we eat it we'll find the spaces and times in combat where it did not work. On the other hand we'll find the spaces where it did work. Then we can reverse engineer and find out why it worked. Were his hands too busy to respond? Was my kick positioned in a way that was out of his line of sight? In doing this we find the times where high kicks would be inappropriate and ineffective as well as the times where it is appropriate. When openings create themselves, it would be inappropriate to respond incorrectly. When it is time for an uppercut, do an uppercut. When it is time for a knee kick, do a knee kick. When it is time for a high kick and we say to ourselves, "Never do a high kick," then we will have missed an opportunity.

Rules are meant to be a guide post for good practice. They guide us to learn and become more efficient. But at times efficiency can actually be sacrificed because we adhere closely to the rules. At this point the rules cease to be a guidepost and become our prison. If we are trapped by the rules, then we have made our own grave. The rules show us the art, but the rules are not the art. If we get caught up in "styles" with "this style does this," and "this style does that," then we limit the potential of the human body.

If we compare all this to painting as an art, first we learn colors, mixing and matching, blending, and what colors go well together. The foundations first are built. Then we start to copy art styles of famous painters to get a feel for how they approach art. And with more examples, we have more to compare and contrast. In time we start to eliminate all the stylistic flare of the other artists and start to find the similarities among them all. We start to see what is the art and what are the personal expressions added by the artist.

Then as time passes we start to create our own art. No longer copying, no longer strictly following rules and staying inside the lines, and instead we break the rules and see how far we can go. This is where our own stylistic expression forms. Martial arts is the same. Eventually we must let go and stop practicing our teacher's art and start to pave our own path. If we only train our teacher's art, we can only be a cheap knock off of our teacher. We must eventually take our own path and take the art further than our teachers. Truly that is the greatest honor you can give a teacher.

Letting Go

Attachments cause suffering. This is the thought behind a lot of Buddhism. The more we attach to things, the more we will suffer for those things. As such Buddhism teaches to let go of desires in order to break free from this suffering. If one has addictions, whether to alcohol, sex, whatever it may be, the more we will long for such things. The more we long for, the more we suffer when we are apart from such things. Also the more we will suffer to bring ourselves closer to that desire. People spend their life's savings on addictions and put themselves into precarious situations. The more we attach to loved ones, the more we hurt when they hurt, and the more we hurt when they are gone. It is important to put our lives into perspective and really ask ourselves, what are we willing to suffer for? What things are worth the sufferings that they bring? That becomes a very important question for ourselves.

25

Sometimes we need to learn to let things go in order to free ourselves of our suffering. The more we hold onto loved ones that have left, the more we will suffer. Instead we should grieve appropriately, let these feelings out instead of bottling them up inside, and let them go in the right timing. The important thing to note are the words, "right timing." To try to let go too early would be akin to a loved one dying and as a response we force ourselves into, "happy mode" mistaking it for, "letting go." When a loved one dies, it is important to grieve. If we don't grieve, we don't express the feelings inside. Those feelings need to be addressed before we can let go. Otherwise we are simply, "putting on a face," but this face is not our true face, so we are only lying to ourselves. We should instead go through the grieving period before attempting to let go and move on. These periods are different for everyone, but everyone must go through these periods for the things they choose to attach to. The lesson to take so far is that it is not bad to attach to things and people, but simply be aware that what we choose to attach to will cause us to suffer.

All of this applies directly to martial arts as well. In martial arts there are many attachments that are made typically. Some are important, many are disruptive to practice. But as practice continues, even the important attachments must be let go. We learn from the textbooks of training, but we must not be slaves to them. We learn many techniques, principles, etc. And it is imperative at first to closely adhere to them as we learn them. Otherwise how would we learn them to the point of making them instinctive? But these things that guided us before will limit our progress as we continue to advance. These rules will bind us in the end. So in true drunken nature, these things must be let go.

If you've ever observed drunkards, you will find that they may still be the same people, but there is something different about them. Alcohol tends to remove people's societal restrictions. Some people were taught and brought themselves up to be quiet and reserved, but you put some drinks in them and suddenly they are chatty and have no concept of personal boundaries. Often this reflects the person inside that is restrained when sober, but the alcohol removes these restraints and lets them move freely.

Drunkards also don't tend to know their own strength. Give them some drinks and suddenly they are strong and feisty like bulls. This is truly what drunken boxing tries to get at. This level of letting go and non-attachment truly brings the potential of the human body. The only difference is that we are trying to get that level of non-attachment while sober. As the saying goes, "Body drunk, Mind sober." We let go and express what is inside, but we do so while also having a sober mind. When drunk, we tend not to have great intelligence and are easily tricked. So having the sober mind is important to not get schooled in a fight. Trying not to go off the rails and lose your mind in the process, but that being said the advanced stages of practice is this idea of letting go. Now that we have foundations and principles to work with, we have plenty to let go.

Let Go of Feeling Power

One of the hardest things to let go of is the need to "feel" one's own power. To do anything else feels counter-intuitive to what one would normally think of as good martial arts. But the key to real power is to let go of needing to feel it. Xu Guoming had a saying. "The tiger doesn't focus on the tiger, he focuses on the prey." It's very true. When hunting, a tiger is not concerned with how it feels when it moves. Its focus is on killing its prey. So why do we hold onto this?

When we tense and flex, we feel strong. So we tend to tense and flex as we fight in an attempt to use this strength, but in reality we are holding that strength inside ourselves. When we tense and flex, we may feel strong, but we restrict our movements and carry our weight. Mass times acceleration equals force. So we need weight to throw and we need to accelerate that weight quickly. So by relaxing we already have seen we can have more potential acceleration, because our movement will be less restricted. But if you've ever held a sleeping baby, you'll know it feels heavier than when it is awake. That's because dead weight is perceived as heavier. When awake they move and start to carry their own weight. So by relaxing, not only do we not restrict acceleration, but we also don't restrict heaviness. So we relax and let our full mass be added to the equation.

Think about a drunk not knowing their own strength. They take a couple drinks and suddenly become monsters. The happy drunk goes in for a hug and nearly splits you in two. The angry drunk gets agitated and clobbers someone with power they didn't know they had. The drunk is not restricted by societal norms and will not hold back for the sake of being proper or following rules. As well they won't be flexing to feel their strength as they swing. A true drunk just doesn't care. This resigned letting go frees the drunk of all the inhibitions holding them back. But this "letting go of power" goes farther than just getting more force and acceleration.

To truly let go of having power means letting go of the need to have power. Many martial artists have trouble getting past the need to feel their force. Even fewer get past this stage into what we are about to talk about. When we get to this point of now having acceleration and mass, we get to this point where we actually know what it is like to have power. We must let go of this too. Once we have this power, we start to use it to fuel all of our movements. Finding the maximum force we can get from each move. This becomes addicting. We start to get this idea of gaining power and become power hungry. In this state we are looking for the most amount of power for each move which becomes an assumption that we can always have our perfect scenario.

Let's be realistic. No scenario is perfect. We can't always have that perfect position. Combat is too chaotic for that to happen. This is where we see drunken boxing in all its weird positions and we think, "how can they have power there?" Drunken again is an exaggeration of the principles. Finding the extent of our range of motion and finding how awkward we can make things for ourselves and still have power. But to talk about this further, does every single movement need to have maximum power? Ideally we'll have maximum power for the position, but not every blow needs to be a killing blow. We look at a position in drunken and think it lacks maximum power, but maybe it has another purpose. Looking at boxing you see small jabs followed by power punches. Those jabs weren't supposed to be knockout blows. If they happen to knock out the opponent, great. But jabs are meant to force reactions, get their attention somewhere else to open them up for a bigger attack. If we only ever think about power, we limit ourselves to potential opportunities. We can't always hit that perfect position, so drunken finds all those positions where we think there is no power and trains there. Maybe we won't have maximum power, but hopefully when we are getting our butts kicked and our opponent is putting us in precarious positions that we can find ourselves familiar enough with crappy positioning to save our lives.

  If we can't fight a losing battle, we'll never find our winning one. The more we hold onto power, the more we will lose it when we get rocked. In the process of letting go of power, we achieve it.

Let Go of how it Looks

Everyone, whether they've trained in martial arts or not, have a preconceived picture of what good martial arts should look like. Whether a seasoned veteran or a martial arts fan who only knows of martial arts through Bruce Lee films. With these views, whatever they may be, people tend to try to make their own martial practice emulate their views of what it should look like. Thus we see a lot of fans who emulate Bruce Lee like their hero and they become like cheap Bruce Lee movie knock offs like the many films made after his death to cash in on his name and face. That aside with this idea of martial arts and preconceived views of how it should look there spawns a lot of elitism.

There is so much divide among the martial arts community. People draw lines between styles, lineages, internal and external, etc. People get concerned with their lineage or style being the best and that anything that is or looks different is just crap. But the thing is martial arts can be and look like many things.

First, to quickly clear some misconceptions, there are certainly wrong ways to practice and huge training mistakes, but there are also multiple correct ways to practice. Some examples of preconceived views that are wrong are that martial arts must be crisp, clean, and sharp. There are ways that sharpness is a type of power delivery that can be cultivated, but the example that I am trying to illustrate is a common misconception from beginners that you must tense your muscles for power. This tends to present a clean, crisp look to it, but it leads to a lack of power and effectiveness and leads one to become stiff and brittle. Another common misconception around those outside martial arts is that you have to be able to kick above your head. This likely came from when tae kwon do became popular in the west as it is known for its kicking techniques. While it is good to be able to kick above your head, I have met plenty of martial artists that can barely kick above their waist and I would bet money on them to win fights.

    So there are in fact wrong ways of thinking, but now we must realize that there is not only one way of correct practice. I see it all the time. Internal martial arts practitioners claiming superiority for their internal training methods, people griping about who has the more prominent lineage, and people looking at another's practice thinking, "that looks different than I was taught, it must be a bunch of crap." The thing many don't realise is that styles are an expression of what my teacher now refers to as "the art." Not "the art" as in the artistic side of martial arts, but martial arts as a whole once lineage, style, and all that are stripped away and we are left with the core of what makes it what it is. "The art" is not even limited to just martial arts, but encompasses any practice, hobby, etc. In the end we are all humans just trying to make it through life, taking our own paths along the way. But we all end up in the same place at the end.

In the same way martial arts styles are methods to obtain and train skills relevant to what we are trying to accomplish. In this case, how to beat up humans. "The art" can be looked at as a mountain. Martial styles are paths up the mountain. But anyone who has walked up a mountain knows it is very hard to walk straight up and it is actually more effective to walk at an angle from the top. Thus many walk zig-zags, or encircle the mountain to get to the top. As such the paths will intersect with each other at some point. These intersection points are the clear principles that the two styles intersecting clearly have in common.

We start at the base of the mountain and paths seem to start in very different places. It is easy for beginners to see this large gap as a divide and then develop elitism in favor of their chosen path. As people walk further up the mountain, the mountain gets narrower as it gets closer to the peak. We then start to see that styles differences are not so different after all, and that there are more similarities among styles than differences. Once reaching the peak, you see who was once your competition are now your war buddies and start telling stories and experiences. Then we realise now that the divide is gone that they aren't much different at all and they've ended up in the same place we did.

The more we hold a divide and a preconceived bias, the more we limit ourselves to what we already know. We stop our own progress up the mountain. We shouldn't be concerned with how our martial arts look, or how another's looks. Looks aren't important at all. A punch is a punch in the end. No matter the body of the car, it runs on an engine. Those engines share principles. If we are concerned with the body and forget to build the engine, then all is for nothing. We can always improve our punches through many training methods and body mechanics, but at the end of the day, did the punch work when you hit the guy? If the answer was yes, then it was a good punch.

Let Go of Shape

Shapes in martial arts are moments in time where the power is delivered through a technique and into an opponent. The shape is the moment the technique "finishes." It is not where the power is generated, but simply the means to apply it in a moment. As my teacher put it, "Shapes are not the power, power goes through the shapes." 99% of the technique lies in between the shapes in the transition. That being said, the shapes are the fundamental building blocks for being able to deliver power through. Without building proper shapes, delivering power would do more damage to us than the opponent. Whether my knee is out of alignment causing something to go wrong when contacting the opponent, or punching the opponent with a misaligned wrist causing it to break.

But eventually we have proper shapes, so the time comes to let them go too. To become shapeless. Eventually from learning shapes, we start to work on the transitional moves and realize that every moment of movement should be able to express power through them. Not just the ending shape. The line between shape and transition begins to blur until there is no difference. The end of one move starts the next without cease. The word "shape" is static. Meaning no movement. A cube is a cube, a sphere is a sphere. But we cannot stay in one shape. Any shape we take in martial arts has glaring holes to take advantage of. So we cannot stay a shape long, or we will be found out. So we must let go of shape to become shapeless. Ever moving, never stopping. It's as simple as moving targets being harder to hit. The more we keep in movement, the more we change from one shape to the next, the harder it is to track. Drunken boxing being an advanced stage of martial arts has no real shapes. It has techniques, but at the same time it has no techniques.

    Drunken shows us shapelessness by having no shapes. Which is why it is often taught to people who already know martial arts. A shape can be caught and constricted, so let go of shape. Any moment power can be delivered from anywhere. Shapes eventually constrict possibilities.

Let Go of Form

To let go of form. To become formless. Every style of martial arts has a certain flavor to it. Whether power delivery is more sharp or heavy. Whether one relies on clever techniques and the other brutal forward momentum, they all are martial arts, but will typically be felt as different to an opponent. This is what it's like to have a form, or a way to describe it. Drunken takes away form to look at the advanced concept of formlessness. If something has a form, we can come to understand it. Because animals have forms to them, we can observe them and learn what it is to be like them. We make great strides in our efforts to understand and observe space, but because it is so difficult to observe it, we don't know a lot about it. We can make limited observations, but some of those observations are replaced by new discoveries as we continue to observe in order to understand.

So having an observable form makes it easy to understand us. A simple observation such as, "Is my opponent right handed or left handed," gives us plenty of opportunities to counter play their game. Now you can adapt to avoid their dominant hand. Is the person hyper aggressive? Perhaps I can use that to throw him off balance. Do they like to keep their distance? Maybe I should be more aggressive and take that space away to take him out of his comfort zone.

Every style tends to create these forms and preferences. We drill the same techniques day in and day out and many never think outside of those techniques. The box we are inside must be broken. To let go of form means to let go of such tendencies. In any moment in combat, the situation can change. With this change we must adapt. Today I will be a lefty. Right now I will keep a cautious distance, but as the need arises I will charge forward. The more we change, the harder we are to understand.

Drunken has no form. It has no preference. The opponent can dictate these things for us. The opponent moves, and our response happens just as quick in response to their strategy. "Oh! You want to square off? Cool, I can do that. Oh you want to dance? Sweet! I love dancing! Oops, you tripped over my foot. How clumsy you are."

Drunken does not have form and its mind does not fight. Drunken moves and goes with the flow. And with that flow we end up in a new position. Little things happen along the way. In the words of Bob Ross those are, "Happy little accidents."

Let Go of Root

Root is a concept previously mentioned in this book to explain the idea of making oneself hard to knock off balance. Acting as if we are a tree with roots in the ground, so our opponent's attempts to take us down will be in vain. But this too is something we must let go of. We train it, hone it, let it go. It begins to work itself without our input. That being said, no one is perfect. No one has perfect root. There will be moments in fights where our root will be disturbed by our opponent and we will be fighting uphill to get it back.

The thing about uphill battles is that they are exhausting and difficult. Try fighting while running uphill and anyone will realize that hopelessly exhausted feeling. When we lose root, the first instinct is to regain it, so that we can fight properly again. If I reiterate this idea in simpler words, when the opponent takes our balance, our first instinct is to regain it and get into a proper fighting position.

But if we think about the fact that this is happening during a fight, then we see the true problem with this.

Anyone who has followed my writings for sometime has probably heard the concept thrown around of taking the balance of the opponent. Because once one has done so, their attention is divided between fighting us and regaining their balance. Once their attention is divided, their brain has begun multitasking. It has been scientifically proven that true multitasking doesn't exist as once your brain has divided its attention, it is not able to function for each task with the efficiency as if it were focusing on one. So once we divide the opponent's attention, it becomes difficult for them to fight back with the same spunk they had before.

So drunken boxing teaches us the concept of letting this go. I'll mention the saying again. "Attachments cause suffering." The more we attach to our root, the more we'll suffer once it's taken. So in drunken, if our opponent takes our root and balance, let them. Don't worry about your root and instead continue following the momentum of the opponent and use it to your advantage. Attach to his limb as he throws you and turn his throw into a break of his limb. As he judo throws you, grab his ear and take it with you. If we are so concerned with not falling over, we aren't fighting them enough.

The "7 steps of the lotus" is the classical stepping pattern of drunken boxing. At first it is an exercise showing how to exaggerate our stepping and positioning to the extreme without falling over. But later we see that the entire art is in those steps. We start a momentum and the momentum takes us through the steps. They become less controlled and more crazy. Whether bigger or smaller steps/movements, the concept is just to move where the momentum guides us, further preparing us to follow an opponent. If we are pushed, our feet will naturally find their way to the spot they need to go to keep us from falling, so trust your training and fight the opponent.

Let Go of Structure

Structure is the backbone of body mechanics in martial arts. Without structure, all our principles of relaxation amount to us lying in a puddle on the floor. Structure being the connected lines and curves throughout the body that allow us to expel and receive force through. We train years to obtain good structure within still postures and then years more to apply them to movement. All to obtain a moving fluid structure. You guessed it. We have to let that go too. But like root, not let go as in throw away, but don't attach to it when it's been taken away.

First to mention, we typically have a rigid view on structure after learning a style as we apply the rules of structure. We like to closely adhere to them to the point anything seemingly outside of those rules can be considered taboo. But what is drunken, but an exaggeration of our orthodox rules. We must be careful not to make the mistake of creating self-imposed limitations. As mentioned previously, drunken seemingly takes precarious positions, but what looks like it is breaking the rules is actually, if done correctly, the furthest extent of that rule. Being able to not stand straight, but have vertical force. Don't be afraid to experiment and test the limits of your art, or you will be bound by your own self-imposed limitations.

I've mentioned already that combat doesn't give us our ideal situation every time. Maybe in solo practice without the chaos of combat intervening we can get that solid structure we were looking for every time, but insert that chaotic element and we can lose it. It would make sense that if having a solid structure makes you difficult to deal with, that the opponent would do everything they can to ruin your structure. And much like losing root or balance, directing your attention to regaining structure divides your attention. So rather than fight for it, go with the flow and see what happens.

Even practice with a partner and when you get to a moment when your structure is taken, freeze and take a moment to see what you can take advantage of instead of struggling to maintain yourself. While in one instance the opponent may bend us over backward, but perhaps that momentum could fuel a nice uppercut if we don't stop to fight it. It's good to have structure, but don't attach so hard that you lose sight of the rest of the fight. Let go and free yourself from the attachment that restrains you.

Let go of Control/Self

Letting go of the self. A concept not unknown to many practitioners of meditation. To let go of the "self," is to let go of our perception of our "self" in order to allow our "true self" to come forward. The concept goes as when we are born, we are our true selves. It is this "self" that some may label as your spirit. But as we go through life, we accumulate many experiences and this changes our outlook on life. Some of us may grow up with abusive parents, and this may lead to a change in thinking about one's own self worth. One may also experience betrayals of many kinds which lead to trust issues. While there are untrustworthy people out there, these trust issues won't pick and choose, but will more than likely sway one into thinking no one else can be trusted. It is tragic to see things like this. It is these very things that also distort our views of reality and truth.

Our own experiences create biases in ourselves that more times than not distort the truth of the matter, or at the very least give us half-truths. One who lies a lot often suspects people of lying, because they reflect their own ego, or perception of themselves, onto others. Sometimes they may be right, but other times not. The ego, or personal bias, is like a window. We are stuck in a room with no way to look outside, but this window. At first it is clear and we can see perfectly. But over time phlegm and dirt will accumulate on the window. These are the experiences that lead to bias. Eventually we won't be able to see clearly what was once clear. To a paranoid person perhaps what was once a view of a tree is now a ghost or a demon. Eventually through the ego we stop seeing what is there and start seeing what we want. This can come in many ways like confirmation bias. Confirmation bias is the idea of looking through information to confirm one's own beliefs. This kind of thing leads to skimming over the full info to find something that may not even confirm their bias, but taken out of context even then supports their argument.

      Thus many meditative practices work on removing the bias from our views and quieting down the "acquired self," in order to allow the true self that usually sits back as an observer of the self, to come forward. To remove all hints of bias, find out who we really are and remove all the bias from our thoughts in order to look at things objectively and see the full truth. Not just one side. To let go of the acquired self in short, is not buying our own self-printed headlines. Not everything we think is right. So we shouldn't just trust our bias.

      In martial arts we like to assert ourselves onto the situation. Assert our structure, assert our techniques in an attempt to control ourselves and the opponent. This is the basic objective of martial arts and it isn't incorrect, but it isn't the "full" right answer. It is only a half truth. The other side of the truth is that you can't control anyone. Chaos assures that we can't always get our way. If we assert our technique and the opponent changes to counter, if we keep trying to assert that technique we are going to eat it. In the same way we must understand that there are moments when attempting to control the opponent will fail. There are moments when we try to control our own movement, but we will fail. If we hold on to this biased view that I can always control the situation, then our ego will be humbled very quickly when we realise that's not always the case. "Everyone has a plan until they get punched in the face," or so the saying goes.

      Drunken teaches us to let go of the "self." To let go of our bias and the need to assert our way. Instead drunken teaches to completely lose oneself into the movement and momentum of the opponent. It is difficult to swim against a flowing river, so use the current to come to the destination you need. Let the opponent dictate how you will beat him. Don't assert your own way. Be polite and listen to his biased opinion and use it to tear him apart. Use their techniques to destroy them with, "happy little accidents."

      The more we hold onto our "self," the more pain we will find whether from an enemy who cares nothing about your techniques, or that of our "self," limiting our growth by ignoring the side of truth that is unpleasant or contradicting our opinions of truth. Let go of the self, look at things as they truly are, not as we wish them to be, and watch the opponent dictate his own destruction using your body as the tool. Don't try, let go and be. Or in the wise words of master yoda, "Do or do not, there is no try."

Let go of mind/body

When we start our practice, we typically have a lack of mind/body connection. Society has a knack for getting us to live outside our flesh in the world around us. Life is too fast paced to just sit down and enjoy one's tea. Gotta drink it on the way to the office. We may not like to admit it, because it is easier to just say, "I don't have time to do things," but we actually have a lot more time than we think. Those that use this time wisely use it to better themselves in practices such as these.

Through these practices we try to integrate the mind into the body as we practice. In martial arts we typically use muscles that are normally ignored and thus it is difficult at first to "find" those muscles in order to teach ourselves to use them. So we place our mind's attention in the spot where the muscle should be in order to try to move and feel that area moving so we know we are on the right track. We continue using our mind to check in with the relationships of movement, structure, etc. to make sure whether we have it or still have further work to do.

But after countless hours of practice, these relationships solidify into the body's instinct and arise naturally. It would be unwise at this point to keep the mind there as it is no longer needed to do so. We brought in the mind, integrated it into the flesh, and used it to work on the relationships. But now that the relationships are trained, we no longer need to place our mind on those relationships. This frees up our mind to work on the next big task now that our body functions on its own. They say internal arts work on internal first and then move to external. As such our mind now must work on the space surrounding us rather than the body itself.

If we take this in levels, first we work on the body in the beginning level. Next we work outward toward the opponent in the intermediate level. This is where most people end up. It is also where most people start teaching. The advanced level the mind moves further outward toward the space surrounding us. Not just the opponent himself. Using the concept of mind over matter, whatever we think with our mind, our body naturally tends to try and follow. As we reach outward with our mind and try to connect with the space, our body is affected as it tries to reach to meet our mind. While the outward appearance may not change, the feeling and quality of touch in the practitioner will. Very few practitioners make it this far. First you have to get lucky enough to find a teacher who has made it this far. Then they have to have the mind of a teacher enough to teach you the foundations of how they got there. Some who have made it there try to teach, but they teach these advanced concepts without first building the foundations, so the student gets nothing out of the practice. It is a matter of the teacher needing to teach the student where the student is in training, not where the teacher himself is.

Without a good teacher it is not entirely impossible as one can get lucky and find themselves at the principles with enough dedication, but it would essentially be recreating the wheel.

Integration of this "spacial power" without the foundations in place will only break the student's chance of success. And without proper monitoring, it is even more difficult to make it, so for the purpose of this book talking about advanced martial arts topics I wanted to mention this practice, but I will not be going over the methods in this book.

The important takeaway here is that in the spirit of letting go, we must let go of the mind/body relationship. It is not as if we will lose the ability to have this mind/body communication, but if we attach to it, it will prevent us from taking the next step in training. We start training, we train principles, we attach to them, we let them go. This is the nature of training and the spirit of the practice of letting go. Nothing stays the same forever. Everything must change and grow. Otherwise we won't train, we won't grow, we will be the same forever. Stagnant. We don't drink from a creek that is stagnant, but from one that flows. Unless of course you like to get sick.

First there is Shape, Let Go of Shape, There Never was a Shape

We start training and we have no shapes. We start training foundations and building shapes to use. We train and eventually we train to let go of these shapes. The shapes meld into the movement. Eventually we train as if there never was a shape.

From wuji, comes taiji. From no shape comes shape. From taiji comes the ten thousand things. From the ten thousand things we go back to taiji. We gain many shapes and principles only to let them go. Taiji then returns to wuji. We return to "no shape." The more we train, the more our shape and structure should become amorphous. No more clearly defined lines and structure. Structure becomes more fluid and while not losing its mass, it becomes more changeable.

Drunken boxing teaches us to extend our definable shape into the undefinable. An opponent should be able to touch us, but not find what we are about. Like water, you can touch it, but you can't grasp it. Before we become amorphous, we are unintentionally honest about our intentions. From a touch you can tell if an opponent is strong or weak. Skilled or unskilled. Stiff or soft. Cautious or blunt. Light as a feather or heavy as a mountain. But to touch the amorphous is to touch a mountain and think it is water. To touch the soft and think it is weak. To touch the blunt and think they are overly cautious.

It is a very common saying now, "to know your enemy and to know oneself, you need not fear the result of 100 battles.," Sun Tzu stated. So to fool the enemy to make them think that you are something else when that is in fact a lie, the enemy walks into battle over confident and unprepared.

Even with a smart opponent, they should never fully understand what they are fighting. If they do not fall for the initial lie, then they are gathering intelligence throughout the fight, but the amorphous should have changed between 3 other ideas before the opponent guesses the first. Change faster than they adapt and victory is within grasp. To be mysterious is to be an unseen enemy.

Master Xu Guoming once said, "1st level of martial arts is like a snake. 2nd level is water. Highest level is like steam." To be a snake. To slither and attack quickly. Changeable and hard to grasp and lock with its flexible body. Water is even harder to grasp. Flowing strong and changing. Moving around obstacles and hits like a wave. Steam is ungraspable, but it also has mass. Even though steam may seem to be weightless, it is only a small change away from water. The steam particles have mass, so it isn't weightless. But while it has weight and mass, we cannot grab it, and it completely surrounds us. To be like steam. To surround the enemy while the enemy cannot grasp or see us. To move like steam is the ideal.

But we can't be like steam if we hold onto shape. Let go of shape when it is time to let go of shape. Then we train and come closer to the graspless steam.

Yin/Yang Reversal

    Every system worth its weight tries to complete itself. Otherwise we are left with glaring holes that can be taken advantage of. Chen taiji trains us to be unmovable like a mountain. Yilu, the first form taught, shows this in its moves which are more like wrestling and qin na moves. And the form itself doesn't really have great footwork, but instead focuses on rooting and being able to absorb the force of the opponent. But Erlu the second form taught attempts to fill in the gaps. It includes more punches, kicks, and its footwork is more free and changeable. It brings the root of the mountain and trains to have moving root while giving strikes and practical techniques to round out the fighting repertoire. In Xingyiquan the 5 elements are taught first and they teach us how xingyiquan expresses force. While the 5 elements technically give us all the skills to be successful at Xingyi, the 12 animal movements give us different ways of using the power to round out fighting ability. Whether the more nimble concept of the monkey or the more straightforward trampling of the horse.

    This concept of "completing oneself" can be understood as a "yin/yang reversal." A yin/yang reversal as it states is the change in focus like the change of yin and yang. If you only train one side of the coin, you only get half the picture. If you are a grappler, it is good to study strikes as well so that when you aren't in a situation where you can grapple right away, you can survive long enough to use your favored skills. The same goes vice versa. It is good to specialize, but it is also good to understand one's own limitations and flaws in order to grow and fix ourselves.

Drunken boxing for many systems is looked at as a yin/yang reversal. It would be why you see strong, hard styles like hung gar have drunken sections in their forms. One cannot always be more stable, more powerful, and more aggressive than the opponent. So drunken in this case becomes the yin/yang reversal. To become soft, changeable, less aggressive while still being a hindrance. It is also why my drunken system has a form including a "sober section." A moment when you "sober up," and start orthodox kung fu. To change and adapt faster than the opponent gives us the likely victory. We can't assume the same strategy works every time. A screwdriver is just not a good tool for hammering nails.

It is an important step for training to look at the other side of the coin. It teaches us to adapt and change. Even looking at applications of techniques. We always say for every technique there are infinite possible applications. So instead of stopping at a simple block and strike, what if we used the technique as a throw? What if the opponent was behind us instead of in front? What if it was to counter a throw or a lock? What if we changed the target of the strike? The limitations of the mind expand and the possibilities become endless. Then we truly lose our shape and form to become shapeless and formless. The answers are no longer cookie cutter and are more open to interpretation. When yin and yang are flipped on their head and we see the two extremes, we see all the nearly infinite variations in between.

Yin/Yang Exist Together

So once one has had the chance to experience the extreme polar opposites that are yin and yang, we next have the chance to experience that yin and yang exist together and that without one, we wouldn't have the other. It is also the case that nothing is always yin or yang, but the context changes the relationship. In terms of solidity being yang, a rock would be yang to water, but water would be yang to steam. We would also come to realise that yin and yang are not a duality, but a relationship. Without one, there is no concept of the other. The only reason we have a concept of day is because we have night to contrast it. And more to be said, yin exists within yang and vice versa. In the early morning yang is rising toward its peak as yin diminishes. In the afternoon yang starts to diminish while yin rises. Varying percentages of yin/yang in interchange.

So we learn two seemingly opposites and have the chance to learn all the inbetween. On a scale of 1 to 100, yin would be at one side and yang could be the other. If we cling to one side or the other, we adhere to one number. But if we learn both sides we can see all the numbers in between. But not only the whole numbers, but numbers down to decimal places. 33.3465, 33.3466, 33.3467, and so on. Without both sides, we miss all the space in between and all the nuances.

In fighting, we cannot be only yin. We will be too soft and get smashed through. We cannot be too yang or we will become stiff and brittle. We must be willing to change. Become yin when the occasion arises, change to yang when the situation changes. But it is not as black and white as that. Yin and yang happen together. So perhaps a receiving block will be yin while the intercepting strike will be yang. The legs generating force would become yang while the torso sinks downward as yin. But one of those legs may be receiving force as yin while the other initiates power as yang. Things start to get complicated as we break it down. But it is important to become complicated before we can let go of the complications.

We learn yin/yang, we then understand its relationship. Then we start to break things down further. Finding nuances of yin/yang. Going even further to understand yin/yang is all context and yin and yang constantly change as they become one another. Yin/yang helps us learn the nuances of martial arts and ourselves.

Yin/Yang Disappear

Yin/yang itself is let go. We learn all that yin/yang has to teach us, and then we let it go and return to wuji. We go from extremity to no extremity. But it is not simply "nothing," but it is a constant potential. The potential to become whatever one needs to be. This state we no longer "decide" between yin/yang decisions. They happen on their own and the answer comes from spontaneity. We do not think about doing. We just do. Everything we train becomes instinct.

We have simply returned to our original state. Before we train, we rely solely on instinct. (Our instincts just suck). We train and learn yin and yang. Then we learn why it is yin/yang, not yin and yang. We understand the nuances and the relationship. We let go of yin/yang and we return once again on our instincts. (Which are trained now). A tree does not try to be a tree, it just is. A tiger does not try to be a tiger, it just is. The ten thousand things return to wuji.

The opponent may try to defeat us, but we present no extremity for him to grasp. We follow the flow of change and adaptation and his own decisions become his own undoing. I do not "do" to him, but he "does" through me. Karma always comes back to bite through our own actions. You attack a tiger, karma doesn't have to explain why that comes back to bite you.

There are 8 Immortals

The 8 immortals in drunken boxing are often depicted as movements of drunken boxing that reflect the personalities of the immortals. While there are moves in the system I study that reflect the immortals, it is more like they are pointing at the concept of each immortal rather than the movements belonging to one or another immortal. The immortals are more like archetypes that you can become. Almost like roleplay. Much like shaolin animal styles, it is not simply having moves that resemble a tiger, but the mind changes as well. Tiger is predatorial. The horse is big, strong, and tramples to defend its life. With these different "personalities" the quality of movement changes. Tiger boxing has more of an aggressive quality when compared to a mantis which is also a predator, but is more cautious.

The 8 immortals affect the quality of movement in this way with the personalities of the immortals giving flavor to the movements. I would like to go over and explain the archetypes briefly, but if you would like to learn about this topic in more detail, I would highly suggest my teacher's book "The Secrets of Drunken Boxing: The Eight Immortals" by Neil Ripski. It goes over the topic in greater detail than I will go over here.

Lu Dong Bin

The leader of the eight immortals and disciple of Zhang Guo Lao. He is known for his invisible demon-slaying sword. He is restrained and exact. He does nothing more than what is necessary. If possible he would do all he could to avoid the fighting and would rather make the opponent submit so no more violence is needed. But if violence is necessary, he is very straightforward and precise.

He Xian Gu

The female of the eight immortals. She acts as the mother keeping the other immortals in line. She fights like fending off gropers. Quick, sharp motions. Unable to be grasped. Loves her elbow strikes and uses physics in her movements to make up for the lack of strength.

Li Tie Guai

Depicted as a lame begger, Li was once a hermit who left his physical body to travel astrally and when he returned, his student who had thought he would never return had cremated his body. Having no choice he looked around to find the body of a recently deceased beggar with one leg and inhabited it. When drunk Li is reminded of his crappy situation he gets angry. Doing drunken boxing while in the mindset of Li, it is not exactly anger, but a disdain for his own situation and he is taking it out on others. Moving as Li is more destructive and uncaring. You are punishing the opponent for picking a fight with you.

Cao Guo Jiu

Depicted as the most sober of the eight immortals, Uncle Cao is a mean-spirited corrupt police officer who delighted in inflicting pain on criminals. He would fight with a lot of Qin Na, restraints and holds like a well-trained officer, but he would take it farther than he should. Whatever he could do to make them suffer a little more.

Zhong Li Quan (Han Zhong Li)

Han was a large man with a round belly who was a general. He is experienced through his time in the military and practical. He likes to utilize throwing techniques to use his size properly. To move like Han would be practical, pragmatic, and using one's own body weight to the maximum effect.

Han Xiang Zi

The pretty boy showoff of the group. Depicted as a handsome young flute player. He is very light on his feet and fights in a way so he can make the opponent look stupid and himself look good. Almost dance-like. He'd fight and show-off at the same time.

Lan Cai He

It is not known whether Lan is male or female, but is depicted as a cross dressing beggar carrying a basket of flowers. Lan is child-like, playful and eccentric, but strong. The kind of drunk who does not know their own strength. Truly a fighter of "happy little accidents." But he is not trying to hurt them.

Zhang Guo Lao

Zhang is the old man and teacher to Lu Dong Bin. He is the immortal that was already an immortal to begin with. Being an old man, he doesn't want to waste any motions. He would fight with as little motion as possible. Less is more. But his mind is that he's teaching the opponent a lesson. Hoping the opponent would learn from the experience.

All these different archetypes are flavorings to add to movements and techniques. It does not matter what technique. They could all do the same wrist lock. Li Tie Guai would hit the lock and then blow through the guy's wrist. Lu Dong Bin would only inflict enough pressure to make the guy submit. Lan Cai He might set up the lock and get excited and start jumping up and down unintentionally breaking the guy's wrist under his body weight. Every immortal essentially gives us another lens to look at our kung fu through. In practicing all eight we get eight possibilities for even one technique. With each outlook, more insight and the clearer the picture becomes.

Imitation vs Embodying

Many martial arts revolve around examples in nature that we try to imitate. Any animal style has us trying to imitate the animal, such as tiger boxing getting us to imitate the tiger, or drunken boxing imitating the state of being drunk. But it goes much further than simply imitation. Rather we imitate until we are able to completely embody that in which we imitate.

It is not simply performing movements resembling a tiger, but a transformation. Much like the 8 immortal training, we are not simply imitating people, but it is more like a transformation. Using the tiger example, it is not looking like a tiger. It is moving as a tiger, thinking as a tiger, becoming a tiger. Moving like a tiger is not literally crawling on all fours, nor making tiger shapes, but the essence of being a tiger. Moving from the spine, the body is soft, but heavy. Moves like stalking a prey. Advancing is like leaping on the prey. The movements and techniques assist us in climbing the prey and pinning them. We don't look at them as rivals or enemies, but food and we are just surviving.

We do not imitate a drunk by bending over backwards and pretending we are drinking. That is the beginning of learning. Instead we embody what it means to be drunk while keeping our minds sober. Relaxed, constant state of falling over, not being rigid in thought, removed societal constraints.

When we apply the 8 immortals, we embody who they are. Cripple Li the bitter drunk, Lan Cai He the playful drunk who doesn't know his strength, Zhang Guo Lao the old man who is a teacher, but is too old to waste more energy than necessary. We don't simply pretend, but for a moment you are not yourself, but something else. My teacher referred to one of his old teachers in a way that describes this well. "My teacher is not a human pretending to be a tiger. He's a tiger pretending to be a man."

There are 9 Immortals

With all these different outlooks and lenses to look through, it begins to shine light onto ourselves and how we perceive reality. We can start to sift through our own bias and strip away the layers of crap until the 9th immortal is finally revealed. The 9th immortal is you. It is easy to go through life only looking at half of anything and begin to form one's opinions based on those limited experiences. But those limited experiences are not our true selves, but our collected experience. The 8 immortals training being essentially role play gives us 8 personalities to imitate and contrast between each other. From these eight experiences we can look at the different aspects they possess and think, "This is nice, but it's not me." And we may look at another and think, "This is more similar to how I think, but it is still not completely me."

It is through the process of seeing the many sides and aspects that we begin to see the many sides and aspects to the self. If we try to pinpoint ourselves before we learn the many aspects, we'll see a one-sided version of ourselves that is filled with a biased outlook. One may see this in practitioners who swear by one martial style alone and look down on those who branch out. They see one aspect and that becomes their personal truth, which closes their mind to the other equally viable aspects.

You could say all of martial training comes out in the end to finding ourselves. Many get caught along the way into what they think themselves to be, or wishing to be like their teachers and the masters of old, but they miss the point. We cannot be our teachers. We cannot be the masters of old. We can only be ourselves. So the path is the way of self-cultivation.

There is only One Immortal

In the end, we can only be ourselves, and this training is to work on the self. Eventually in practice we have to stop imitating others and start doing our own art. In the beginning it can be detrimental to try to put oneself in the style, because at first we must use the process of imitation to learn new things. We must first learn and feel "why" our teacher tells us, "it is this way." When we are lost in the woods, we should listen to the man with the map. But eventually it is time to do our own art. Eventually we've walked these woods enough times to not need a map. It does not mean we stop listening to our teacher. From time to time we still lose our way. Especially when treading new ground. But our teacher cannot be relied on forever. Because once they are gone, we will be forever lost.

In the many stages of Nei Gong (literally "inside work," or character work) we shed off the layers of fat which obscure our true self to bring it forward. This self then influences everything we do. It is not a simple, "I change this move, because I like this better." Changes happen rather in a passive way, or as a result of the training. Once we find our true self that has been buried under bias, it can finally give uninhibited input. Changes happen to our system on their own from our now unbiased experiences. This is where our true art is expressed.

Nei gong is an extremely underrated part of martial arts training, and to be fair, at first it sounds like a bunch of hippy nonsense. What possible use could character work give for martial arts? Well things like trauma come up a lot in martial arts. Fear is a major driving force for humans, but fear stiffens us, slows reactions, and even affects how we react. By working on the self and dealing with the fear-involved trauma, it can lead to letting such things go, so our reactions are smart and appropriate. To let go of sad events let us unravel all the tension held deep within our bodies that inhibit us from relaxing and sinking. To deal with our own angry habits makes it so that anger will not overcome us in battle and blind us.

We can see with this how character work and martial arts are intertwined. If we only focus on physical techniques, then we will be limited by those techniques. So we must not neglect the cultivation of the 9th immortal. Ourselves. On the road to becoming a better person, we become a better martial artist as a side bonus.

Rule of Xu: Everybody Sucks, do the Opposite

Xu GuoMing (George Xu) is by far one of the best martial artists I have ever met. His power is like that of a tsunami, he is light like steam, heavy like a mountain, and moves like an animal. My teacher was talking with him one day and asked him how he got this way. He responded, "Everybody sucks, so look at what they do and do the opposite." This certainly isn't the most politically correct thing to say, but now I can say from plenty of experience in applying this rule of thumb that it is quite useful. How would we have the technological advances that we have today if not for learning from the failures of the past.

In most things, there is an 80/20 rule that 20% of people who do any practice or profession are really good at it, and 80% are meh, or below average. In martial arts this tends to be even more. About 10% actually get good. This is likely due to martial arts being such a niche interest. But even more so, 1% of those actually become martial titans. This tells us that there are far more bad examples, or examples of average martial arts than good ones. So this rule ensures that the 90% of people we run into, we can still learn from them, even if it is what not to do.

So let's look at some things and apply the "Rule of Xu." People like to fight over lineage wars and use lineage as social influence or clout. So we must be humble and not drag our ancestors' corpses around for clout. People like to "make stops" after techniques with crisp movements. So we must flow, and not stop. People like to tense their muscles upon impact, so we must relax, be heavy, and hit through the opponent. Some people like to only train the soft sides of the art while others cling to the hard, so we must balance the training. People like to get caught up in the style vs style debate, so we must move past this. Some like to train all the time and neglect rest while others hardly train. So we must balance our time wisely. People like to focus on speed and strength, so we must work on the lazy path. Get the most power with the least effort and become efficient. People like to live in their comfort zone, so we must tread new paths. People like to adhere to their lineage and teachers so much that they try to be copies of them, so we must become our own masterpieces.

    No matter who is in front of us, we can learn from them. If we only take the good experiences, then we only take 10% of our opportunities to learn. If we train like everyone else, then we will just be like everyone else. For many they consider it to be taboo to change anything or to tread new ground with their art as they think it is insulting to the ancestors who passed down the art. But in reality, to take a teacher's work even farther than they themselves could go is the greatest compliment. If you look at any of the big names in the martial arts, they became big names because they treaded new ground. Dong Hai Chuan, Cheng Ting Hua, Hung Hei Gung, Chen Wang Ting, Sun Lutang, Chen Fa Ke the list goes on of the many legendary names. But they all share in common that they took what their teachers taught and expanded upon it. Creating new styles or heavily influencing the style until it becomes something different.

    In the end, we aren't learning styles, we are learning martial arts. Styles are a collection of methods to obtain skills, they are not the skills. So let us apply the rule of Xu again. People train to master the style. So instead we master "the art." We eventually must strip away and let go of "the style" that restricts us and look at the core of things. The style helps us get to the core, but it is not the core.

Change the Self

Neigong is the practice of working on the "self." Who we are. Self-cultivation. There are many aspects that make up the self, and none of them should be neglected. Many tend to think of the "self" as specifically their consciousness or mind, but this is not complete. Many talk about our "self" being a brain accompanied by nerves piloting a mech suite of bones and flesh, but not one individual part of this is the self, but the culmination of the parts are the self. We do not have a mind and body. We have a mind/body.

Below I will list and define the 5 stages of Neigong practice, what they do, and how they relate to the practice.

1. **Moving the 4 big joints**

    The first stage of self-cultivation is to mobilize and exercise the 4 main joints of the body. Both hips and both shoulders. Without motion, we are not alive. Even when we are still, blood moves. When movement comes to a stop, we die. So the first step is to move. The more we move, the more healthy we become and the less pain from stiffness we will have. This can be looked at as a young animal learning to crawl. In this stage we integrate the mind deeply into the flesh as we like to treat the mind and body as separate things, so we end up living outside of our flesh in our daily lives. This stage starts to regain the mind/body relationship.

2. **Learn to stand**

    This stage usually is accompanied by standing practice like standing post and other meditative exercises. We learn and integrate further into our flesh making micro adjustments in our posture. This stage is about changing our reflection of our self. We often hide our true self behind a wall in order to become someone else. Either to fit in with social norms or we simply are not happy with who we are, so we try to change who we are. Oftentimes we don't even realize this about ourselves, like in the case of those growing up in a household strong in beliefs in one way or another. And as we grow, we tend to become more like those around us. But as we start to chip away at the influences of those around us, we start to find that perhaps we don't agree on such things after all. So in this standing practice, we are "literally" finding where we stand in the universe. We stand and find our true selves.

3. Finding the earth

Also accompanied well with standing practice. In the last stage we talked about who we are, now we try in this stage to find "where" we are. As we continue standing, we release and relax the flesh from your upper body, through your lower body. We feel the weight of our flesh and let it sink until it hits the floor through the bottoms of our feet. And through the laws of physics, we know if we push the earth, it pushes back. As our weight hits the earth, the earth pushes back. We feel the earth under our feet. We start to ground ourselves in the earth. This stage is about grounding ourselves in reality. As we feel the earth, we find where on the earth we are. We are seeing where we fit into reality.

4. How we interact with the universe

Now that we've found where we are, we start to observe our interaction with things around us. Picking up things, touching people. Observe your interaction with touching people and touching their mind. This stage is how you treat the things around us. We find that there are more to things than one's initial interpretations. Animals are alive. Plants are alive. They breathe and feel. It's easy to forget. That person we yelled at last week is a human with feelings, a family, dreams and goals. This is a stage where we learn how necessary compassion is.

5. Action-non-action

Not striving, yet not leaving anything undone. Putting the mind in the present moment and not worrying about the end result. It is easy to get stuck with thoughts of the future and become anxious as well as thoughts of the past leading to depression. The past is done and no longer exists. The future hasn't happened and therefore doesn't exist. As Christians often put it, we make plans and God laughs. The only moment that exists is right now. Learning to be in the present moment and letting go of that which no longer matters. Do or do not.

As we can see, the first three stages are about finding our self and grounding ourselves in our flesh. It is easy to fail at these stages and many are led astray by this seemingly hippy nonsense. But it is important to grow as a human. But in order to interact properly with others, or have compassion for others, first we must find and have compassion for ourselves. Without first integrating the mind/body, one can lose their mind and float away. The flesh is the anchor of the mind.

Thus the last two stages are about interacting with all that surrounds you. How you interact with things or behave with people. Not getting lost or trapped by things that we can't help or change. In letting these things go, your spirit will be freed, and your true self can be expressed without obstruction. Once again, we are tasked with letting go.

Emptiness

Emptiness is a concept of buddhism and high level martial arts practice. To look at it in Buddhism for a moment, on the path to enlightenment we will be given questions to ponder. My teacher gave me some of these questions to ponder for my martial arts practice and my self work. Normally the question is given and the student is left to figure it out for themselves, but I think for the purpose of this book I will give more discussion to the topic than simply say, "practice."

The first question he gave me was as follows. "Point at your nose." I proceeded to point at my nose. "Why did you point there at the center bridge of your nose? Why not higher or to the side?" I was a bit puzzled. "Meditate on this question for a couple weeks. What differentiates the bridge of your nose from the rest of your nose?"

I left puzzled, but I did as he said and I meditated on it daily. Over time the answer uncovered itself. I came back to my teacher and said that I couldn't find a differentiation. When you look at things very broadly, things can seem to have differentiation, but the closer I looked at a cellular level there is no differentiation between the bridge and the rest of my nose.

He then gave me more questions to ponder. "Who/what are you? Are you your leg? Your arm? Are you the emotions you feel? Are you your anxieties? Your thoughts? Your spirit? Your mind? Your body?"

I meditated on these questions for another couple weeks. After coming back I asked my teacher, "Am I not any one thing?" Essentially he told me that this training is to remove false preconceptions about ourselves. The common way people look at themselves today is a brain and a series of nerves piloting a meat suit. But the truth is that our meat and bones are not any less "us" than our brain. But at the same time what isn't us?

In buddhism it is said that everything is made of grains of sand (later found to be atoms). If we look closely enough we will find those grains. But what is between the grains of sand? Emptiness. Not nothingness. Nothing doesn't truly exist beyond a concept. But between the sand there is emptiness. So all we are is atoms and emptiness. And all things in existence are atoms and emptiness. So truly what is the difference between us and another. Between us and a shelf. The closer we look, the less there is a difference.

Self vs Non Self

So this chapter on emptiness kind of sounds like it contradicts the idea of finding true self. Finding no differentiation between our self and another kind of gets rid of the idea of self entirely. The truth is both are true. We do have a self that is unique to us, but also simultaneously there is no difference between ourselves and another. This is another paradox to ponder.

The key is to understand that while we are unique, we are also the same as those around us. The concept of racism exists because of the fear of things that are different from us which creates tribalism and division. In one form or another division has existed since the beginning of time and will continue to exist in the future. But with the teaching of emptiness we learn to look at everything as important. Regardless of beliefs, looks, personalities, we are all made up of the same stuff. We all go through hardships, loss, hunger, happy times, etc. So while we are different, we are inherently the same. Same as animals, plants and the like. They are just trying to survive, eat, and reproduce. Perhaps we can have more compassion for those around us if we realize everyone is just like us.

Emptiness and Martial Arts

Emptiness is important for martial arts practice. From an internal to a combative perspective, Removing the concept of self removes limitations we put on ourselves unknowingly. When throwing a punch for example, one of the beginning stages of training this concept is hitting past a target. This also has to do with the idea of letting go of the opponent's sense of self. Rather than trying to "hit a target" you are simply swinging your body through space and the poor sucker happens to be in the way. This concept allows one to hit with considerable penetrating force.

But in order to do this properly, there is something else to consider. This is where martial arts can get weird. One step off the path leads thousands of miles in the wrong direction. This is where you get fake masters who do no-touch knockouts and the like. One simple mistranslation and everything is lost. This is why having a knowledgeable teacher is important to keep you on track. So looking back at the earlier example of reaching past a target rather than hitting a target. This begins the mind reaching past the body training which increases the force one will output. Psychological change results in physiological response. But this again is the beginning stage. From the example, the power comes from within the body and moves outward all as a result of the mind. But the advanced stage of this is using the mind to use power from the space around you, not limited to your own body.

    This is not literal and not magic Qi lasers, though that would be really cool. It's just another mind change which affects the body's response. If I'm throwing a hook punch for example, instead of thinking to reach through the arm as I hit, I instead imagine the whole room turning. This again results in a bigger power. It sounds like a bunch of garbage and I thought so too until I got hit with it. But if we look at everyday examples, we can see plenty of circumstances where a change of mind intent naturally changes how our body responds. When someone is feeling good and confident, their posture tends to straighten up and people can feel this confidence coming off of them. And when we are talking to someone we might be crushing on, without even noticing we might find ourselves a little closer to them with our bodies facing toward them as opposed to when we are approached by a sketchy stranger and our body posture closes off to them. Mind affects the matter.

    So the concept of emptiness in this case refers to the idea of letting go of our physical body in a sense. After we train the physical body to the point where our body can do the movement principles without conscious thought, our mind doesn't have to focus on it anymore and our bodies run on autopilot. This frees up our mind to connect to the space around us. It's the idea of letting go of our "self" and realizing that the space around me is just as much me as my body is. So now you move your "self," but your "self" is no longer your physical body, but the space you reside in.

But training like this is quite difficult and I don't suggest trying it without a teacher who really knows it and having their close guidance. Otherwise we may end up on some fake martial masters video on youtube.

Emptiness and Drunken Boxing

Much like emptiness removes the defining lines between ourselves and other things. Drunken boxing removes the defining lines we like to draw as to what is and isn't martial arts. We all have biases and beliefs about things. And those of us trying to grow try to remove these biases and limitations we put on ourselves. Such biases like martial arts are precise. Drunken boxing doesn't care as much about precision. Drunken boxing is much like flinging your body through the air, and if someone happens to be in the way it is not the practitioner's problem. Happy little accidents as it were.

Another bias can be that martial arts teaches you perfect positioning. This is true, but not all the time. Nothing is perfect and those of us that only train under perfect positioning tend to eat fists once we are taken out of perfect positioning. Drunken boxing instead likes to train in those areas of weakness. Training in those areas gives you familiarity. So when later you are put in such a position, you know how to fight there. Covering your weaknesses as it were.

Drunken boxing is the tool we can use to erase those lines we define our world in. The more we hold onto those lines and definitions, the more we will suffer at our own cause. The world isn't black and white and neither is martial arts. First we need the lines as a structure for learning purposes, but eventually we must get rid of those lines. We can't be on training wheels forever. We can't practice our teacher's art forever. Instead, take a few drinks and see what comes out.

Enlightenment: Seeing Things that were there Before

    We often talk about things like enlightenment like it is some other-worldly form of attainment. But in reality, it is more akin to taking off blinders and seeing what's been staring at you in the face our whole lives that we never noticed before. The saying goes, "Before enlightenment, chop wood and carry water. After enlightenment, chop wood and carry water." To treat oneself like they've made a great attainment and are now above others is the exact wrong thing to take from it and further proves such a person is far from enlightenment.

    Instead we take what we learned from the experience and continue our daily lives now knowing what we know. Life doesn't change, but our mind and perception does. Enlightenment is akin to, "waking up." This is where some really weird qigong came out of. Circle walking around a tree to realize they are alive. Standing, watching clouds pass and observing the passage of time. Sitting and listening to the things around you, then sitting and listening to the things inside you. Pretty obvious things to think about, but rarely experienced. Experiences often change our perceptions of things. So by observing through such qigong, we are enlightened to the obvious that we hadn't looked at before. We know through scientific studies that trees are alive, but do we realize that they breathe, feel, communicate. We often take things for granted, but there are so many things to learn from the obvious that will change us forever.

So we obtain these experiences. What next? We continue life, now knowing what we know. And now knowing what we know, likely we will change how we go about that life. We can go walk through the woods, but now we will realize that we are not alone in this world. We trained to listen, now we listen to all around us. But listening is not limited to hearing. We train and observe, we open our minds and learn that there is a lot to learn from this world. Further removing bias to make us into a vessel of learning. Not simply accepting without thought, but not denying without contemplation. Through listening, we find our place in this world.

Enlightenment: Opening the Mind, Changing the Nervous System

The more we open the mind, the more we can learn from this world. But also we allow the nervous system to process information. The mind/body relationship learns together. The nerves pick up information and send it to the brain. The brain deciphers information and responds with the appropriate charge to the nerves to activate the body in response. By listening with one, we work on both.

If we close off our mind to new information, then the body will not develop a proper charge. The mind/body will be stagnant. If we ignore our body relationship, the mind will have difficulty in deciphering information as the mind/body relationship will not be helpful in the process.

The mind teaches the body, and the body teaches the mind. In martial practice, we may watch a movement and attempt to imitate. The mind tries to teach the body to follow suit. Over time of hearing our teachers talk about corrections like aligning the knees, move from the center, etc. eventually we may find our bodies made a sensation. We tell our teachers about it and they may say that the sensation is a good sign that we are on the right track. So now the student has a sensation that he has observed and now it is a matter of practice to get it right while now having an experience to guide our practice. The experience is a result of the body and the bodies' attempt to teach the mind how it works. Without this relationship, it is easy to get lost along the path.

So as we practice and find enlightenments, it is the mind/body relationship attempting to teach us. The more we listen, the more likely we will learn, and the more likely we will learn to listen better. Like learning to listen more in a spousal relationship, we can't become better listeners unless we practice listening. In the process of learning to listen, the bodies' nervous system essentially gets a workout. The more we inhibit it, the worse at processing information we become.

An electrical charge needs a path to travel. If there are blockages, it cannot travel efficiently, and it will use up some of its charge just getting past the obstacle, then becoming a weaker signal. We talk so much about postural alignment as the "physical" representation of this. Relaxing your body so the charge does not get used by being blocked by the muscles. Then the mind must be in a willing state to hear the information as well. A blockage in the mind might be talked about as a "spiritual blockage" or the way I prefer to call it, mental barriers. Mental barriers are self imposed blockages of the mind that denies information. Like when people talk about heated topics such as religion or politics. People tend to say that they are open-minded, but when these topics come up it becomes more of a pissing contest than a discussion where you are trying to hear each other's points. But the more we open our minds to hear what the other has to say, even if we don't agree with them, we can still see they might have solid reasons for believing in what they do and they may be going down a path just as viable as ours. We have to remember, differing opinions can both be right. And even if we don't agree at the end of the day, we are all living creatures just trying to make it through this world. So instead of responding with hostility, we can respond with compassion, listen, and perhaps even learn something that we didn't know or understand before.

    There are two sides to every coin, and both sides are the coin. No individual side is the full coin, but both seemingly different sides are the full coin. We open the mind and change the nervous system, and it makes practice easier to understand. Ting jin or listening power to feel the changes in motion. Or the improved mind/body relationship makes it easier to learn principles and body mechanics, because we are living with our mind integrated into our flesh. Finding muscles in us that we didn't realize were there before, but now can feel as we integrate our mind. Enlightenment man. Seeing stuff that was always there.

Practice a Style, Remove the Style, "The Art" Remains

We don't train styles of martial arts, we train martial arts. We practice a style to gain the skills the style will teach. Styles of martial arts are just methods. Whether doing boxing, mantis, taiji, whatever, the styles teach you how to fight. Some styles may prefer to teach you to fight cautiously like northern mantis while others may teach you to be more aggressive like Xingyi. But at the end of the day, they both teach fighting.

To say we are trying to master a style in particular would be like a carpenter saying he will master the hammer while another will master the saw. Both are used in carpentry, and while it is not wrong to have one's own preferred tools, you'll need to understand all the tools you will be using. This is not to say we must practice all martial arts, but instead of limiting ourselves to one side of the coin we instead get to the core of the matter. The tool does not matter, it is how you use them, and the knowledge of which tools are appropriate for the situation.

So rather than master a style, instead work towards mastering the core of the matter. We can do so by following the paths laid out by the style we practice. We can travel the path of boxing, mma, kung fu, karate, etc. but the core of what we practice is "the art." So we go to learn a martial style, we practice this method and gain knowledge and experience from it. Our foundations are built, principles are defined, body methods are trained. We start to get somewhere. Eventually we take all the techniques and narrow it down to the core concepts. At this point the style becomes smaller and smaller. Eventually the style disappears. Styles that seemed different before are now more similar than different. The concept of "styles" starts to get smaller as we get closer to the core of the matter.

Drunken is very much about removing the "style." First you have style, then you get rid of style, then it is as if there never was a style. Drunken breaks the style's rules and frees the brain from the mental barrier of styles that divide practitioners of martial arts behind their opinions. Without the style restricting your sight, you can begin to see the art itself. You can add flavor to body methods, but the human body is the human body. Fighting is fighting. These are very basic ideas, but it is the core of martial arts as a subject matter for fighting. There is going to be more cross over between styles than differences the closer you get to the heart of the matter.

Let go of the need to be of a style. You practice a style, but you are not the style. Your fighting may resemble the style, but fighting is fighting. How do you wish to cook? Fried, steamed, broiled? If the ingredients are the same, then the thing that is different is the ending taste. But the flavors don't give you the nutrients, the food does. We may prefer certain flavors, but the thing that matters is the sustenance.

Don't Try to be your Teacher, be You

     Many of us have role models that we look up to and try to emulate. For martial arts practitioners it is no different. Some of us tend to look up to our teachers as well as practitioners of the past. It is especially important in the beginning to have our teachers to emulate as at first emulation is the way we learn. And looking to past masters can be great even for advanced practitioners to gain inspiration and direction by analysing the journeys of past masters. But it is important to keep this in moderation. While having a role model can be good, if it moves into the realm of hero worship it can obscure our views of reality.

     We always hear great stories of the masters of the past. But it is often obvious that many of those stories were embellished over time. We can end up getting lost in the fantasy of these stories and put these masters on a pedestal above ourselves and view them as forever out of our reach. Many will think, "I will never be as good as the past masters." This is both a disservice to ourselves and the martial arts. We need to realize that our teachers and the past masters are and were in fact human. They make mistakes and are nowhere close to perfection. I was making jokes during a class I was teaching the other day. My student put his head in his hands shaking his head saying, "The past masters are groaning in their graves seeing us now. What would they think of us?" I turned to him and said, "They would likely act the same way." Humans want to laugh and have fun. It is easy to view past masters as super-enlightened, wise, yoda-like beings, but we should remember that giving them this otherworldly personality of wisdom further distances our view of reality.

  Ranting aside, I believe it is important to mention this to keep our minds on reality. If we separate the past masters from ourselves, then trying to emulate them would be pointless. We as humans would never reach these ideals we made up, and the arts would fade over time as each following generation would continuously fail to emulate and would instead become a lesser copy of our teachers. We cannot be our teachers, and we cannot be the past masters. We can only be ourselves.

  If you look at all the big name martial artists of the past, then you may see a trend. They all took what their teachers gave them and expanded upon it or made something new. It is easy to think that we should strictly adhere to tradition and keep everything as it was, but that would be like pinning a butterfly to study it. Sure you could easily study its shape that way, but you'll never understand what it means to be a butterfly that way. The essence will be lost. Is it not a greater compliment to our teachers to take what they have done and take it even farther? There is no greater accomplishment to a teacher.

Sun LuTang is a big name. He learned Bagua, Xingyi, Taiji and created the Sun system of all three. His bagua teacher Cheng Ting Hua (Cheng bagua founder) even taught him that to be a master of bagua, you must create your own 8 palms. Which Sun Lutang did. This is an important process to see if a student truly understands what you have taught them. Each palm change represents concepts, body methods, principles, and fighting methods. Not only just applications. Each palm change is more than movements. But to truly understand the concepts, it is important to be able to say them in our own words. If our teacher asks what one concept is, and we reply with the exact words like reading it directly from the textbook, do they truly understand what they said, or are they simply regurgitating the information. After one gains the information, to put it in our own words allows our brain to actually process and understand the information. Otherwise we become robots regurgitating information that was fed to us, and when our future students ask us why things are the way they are, we answer with, "because that's the way the teacher did it."

We must ask questions, experiment, pressure test, and ask more questions. This is the way to understanding. Not becoming a yes-man. The process in bagua of creating your own 8 palms is putting your understanding of the concepts out on the field. We can then look to see what we actually know. It's the same as the masters who created their own styles and systems. It is the art that they were shown now expressed through their own minds. Teachers are necessary to come to an understanding, and role models give us inspiration, but if we hold onto them, it hurts our practice. We must learn to let go. It does not mean don't look for or listen to teachers, but not attach to them to the point that it limits our growth. Teachers cannot give us kung fu, they can lead us the way to kung fu, but we must walk that path ourselves. If we attach too much, then we become empty, hollow carbon copies when our teachers pass on. We must let go of the need to be like someone else, and instead be the best version of ourselves that we can be. To find our true self, we must let go of the ego and all else.

      Freedom is something we give to ourselves after we let go of all the things trapping us. We are our own worst enemy. We are our own greatest critics. We live our lives limiting ourselves of our potential, serving as our own prison warden. In order to be free, we must let ourselves be free. We start training and must learn to let go of all our preconceived notions of what training should be in order to allow ourselves to learn. We then build our repertoire and build our foundations off of the principles of what we learn. Then we return to the state of letting go. Coming full circle and returning to the center.

Imitation vs Embodying 2

(You may be wondering why there is a part 2 to this chapter. Well during the construction of this book I ended up taking an extended break from writing. During that time I was with my teacher learning, practicing, and helping him teach some workshops. In this extended break I did my best to further my knowledge and understanding. When I came back to work on this book, I had completely forgotten that I had already written this chapter. So I wrote another version below. Later I realized what I did and was going to remove the old version as the new version I felt gave a more complete answer to what I was writing about, but I eventually decided to keep it. As I have written books and articles in the past, looking back at them is a good way to gauge your knowledge of the past and seeing how much you've improved. I believe this is important for everyone to consider in their own journeys. So for the sake of it, I will include both)

In martial arts there are many "imitation" styles. These styles include Tiger, Mantis, Snake, Drunken, etc. What it means is that these styles find their inspiration from something and they imitate that "something" as they practice their art. Animal systems find their inspiration from… Well, animals. Unlike humans, animals still have their teeth and primitive instincts intact as we have built comfortable lives for ourselves outside of nature where survival is number one. So animal systems imitate the animals in order to tap into and train our long lost primitive instincts. Drunken boxing imitates the constantly relaxed and uncontrolled nature of a drunk person in order to break formalities and rigidness to find the actual limits of our bodies.

But while imitation is a big part of the arts, it is still only the beginner stage. Beginners imitate the source of inspiration and their teachers in order to learn the art and how it works. But pretending is only going to get you so far, and then we will find a plateau in our journey. It is at this point we must learn the differences between imitating and embodying.

Through imitation, we teach ourselves what it means to be that particular thing. Eventually we must stop pretending to be that thing and realize that the training was not to pretend to be the thing, but to become the thing itself. Imitating the tiger until you become the tiger. My teacher always described his teacher in the Ma family arts as not a "man pretending to be a tiger, but a tiger pretending to be a man." The arts go far beyond movements made to look like a tiger, but to becoming the tiger itself. Thinking like a tiger. Moving like one.

Much like the principles of the art, at first we don't know them, so we imitate them until eventually they click and work. Then we begin to embody them as we replace our old untrained instincts with these new principles and make them into our base instinct.

Only then can we take drunken's true lesson and let them go. Without first embodying the principles, we cannot let them go. By letting them go, we can be free of the restrictions that come with the process. Every style has restrictions and rules to teach you to be a certain way as you learn. This is important in order to help you learn the things you must learn at this stage. Then eventually we must let them go. The style starts to disappear and "the art" makes itself known to us. Styles are not the martial arts in themselves. They are systems of thought and training methods to teach you martial arts, but we must not mistake them as the goal in themselves. In any profession, we learn from a teacher/mentor/peer how to do the profession. We may even do outside research with books, etc. But eventually we must put the books down and do the work on our own.

      Through experience and practice we teach the art to ourselves. We start to see that there are ways to do it that are different than we were taught. Maybe even new ways. We begin to explore possibilities as the art reveals itself more and more. This is where we let go of the styles and systems and begin to embody "the art" itself. This is where we start taking up our hatchet and machete and start making new ground. Without our teachers and systems, we wouldn't have made it to this point. Without eventually letting them go, we will not tread this new ground. We must honor them by making this new ground for the next generation.

Conclusion

There are many things to think about and contemplate when it comes to advanced martial practice. But most importantly we must focus on our basics. All advanced practices fall apart without a proper foundation to build off of. All of the advanced practices in reality are not separate things, but extensions of our basics. To get overzealous will only hold back our progress. We must realize that in order to let go of something, we must first pick it up.

That being said, when it is time to let something go, then we must let it go. We mustn't keep holding onto the scalding pot. Before lighting the fire, the pot was not too hot to hold, but once the temperature gets to a boil it would be foolish to hold onto it any longer. Attachments cause suffering. We all must learn this lesson at some point. We are the major cause of our own lack of progress. We like to jump to advanced things before we are ready, and then we can't let things go once it is time to talk about such advanced topics. This is why working on our very "self" is so important.

But as with anything, when lost it is good to seek the help of someone already experienced. Older eyes can help to see our own flaws and then point us in the right direction. It is also important to keep ourselves honest. When alone, it is easy to lie to ourselves. Not so easy in front of someone who knows.

To anyone reading this book who is looking for the next step in their training, I can't recommend enough to find a good teacher. The things I mention in this book are meant to supplement training and open eyes to realize there is a lot more to the path than many of us even realize. This book was not meant as an instructional. So for anyone looking to practice these things, please find a teacher who already has experienced these things. One step in the wrong direction can lead thousands of miles in the wrong direction in time. But that would just be my two cents.

Notes

Notes